50 Leadership Principles PART III:

How to position YOUrself digital for success

By Jorge Zuazola © founder of European Leadership © 23rd July 2019

ISBN: 9781082243035

INDEX

PRINCIPLE #101: Make digital friends not corporate world enemies

Digital people take full responsibility. If you want happy friendships, you have to take digital responsibility. Even if you figure it is your parents fault that got you to a bad start to life, decide that it is up to you to do something now in the digital 4.0 world. **If you don´t fix your life who will ? Nobody can make you miserable without your permission. You decide how you feel.**

PRINCIPLE #102: Be your own digital auditor

Go through the digital auditing process weekly as a habit which includes keeping a daily cash book with the cash in and cash outs electronically. Auditing is a process where an auditor comes in, the financial statements and checkbooks come out, and the details of your digital financial life are reviewed in detail

PRINCIPLE #103: Become self-confident through digital mental picturing

Choose Happiness, Trust Yourself and Picture Your Goals digitally. Self-confidence´ is a general term we use to describe people who are relaxed, successful and self-assured. The mind thinks in mental pictures which means digitalization forms an image maker for us. If you visualize your goals, and self train on it your mind will move you towards then much faster than you think. But you need to do it daily. You are an image maker. Do it daily.

PRINCIPLE #104: Be a digital entrepreneur as we cannot live on a Social Security Pension

Would you argue with this finding now ?
Well before the 2008-09 recession which led
to the current digital revolution, a USA
Today survey discovered that the
Americans´ number one fear is running out
of money. Their number one fear was not
cancer, crime, or nuclear war. Their number
one fear is running out of money in their old
age. The new fear is living a long life
without money. Most people realized then
that Social Security and Medicare may not
even be around to assist them in their old
age.

PRINCIPLE #105: You can never win a digital argument

« There is nothing either good or bad » said Shakesperare « but thinking makes it so ». Therefore there is no point in arguing digitally with anbody. You can´t win an argument in the digital economy. You can´t because if you lose it, you lose it ; and if you win it, you lose it. Why ? Well suppose you triumph over the other man and shoot his argument full of holes and digitally prove that he is non compos mentis. Then what ? You will feel fine but what about him ? You have made him feel inferior. You have hurt his pride. He will resent your triumph and « A man convinced against his will is of the same opinion still »

PRINCIPLE #106: Seek wisdom besides digital education

Many people mistake digital intelligence for wisdom. But being smart digitally does not make you wise. There are many people in this world with Mensa-level IQs, but with little or now wisdom. When it comes to making wise decisions about digital relationships or morality, they are utterly clueless. A university degree in philosophy is not enough to make you wise. No one ever became wise by watching television, going to the movies or surfing the Internet. Some people say that wisdom comes with experience. Yet many people are very experienced yet also very foolish. Clearly, experience alone doesn´t make a person wise. True wisdom is the result of deliberate choices we make. No one acquires wisdom by accident. Wisdom must be desired,

PRINCIPLE #107: Your digital profitability is your priority

We have all heard the rule " pay yourself first" but it is tough to do when your income does not exceed your expenses. **Digital Profitability is the first priority.** Once you have cut your expenses and have money left over, you need to start saving immediately. Save as much money as you can, at an early age as possible, and invest it well.

PRINCIPLE #108: Spend 20 minutes a day on digital goal achievement

Your digital goals should be an ever-present part of your life, offering you direction and encouragement. Don´t come up with a list of goals, hide them away somewhere, and check back forty years later to see if you reached them. Create them, use them, follow them, update them live by them **Successful people spend at least 20 minutes every day thinking about what they are doing and can do to improve their lives.**

PRINCIPLE #109: Have digital tenacity and capacity of sacrifice

Leaders like winners. They admire their effort, their tennacity, their sacrifice capacity, their willingness to set objectives and achieve them. I would like that Spain was a country of winners, and not because there are not may people capable to succeed, in fact there are, but because frequently the Spanish people do not recognise the merit which corresponds to the succesful people who has been able to reach the excellence through their talent and hard work. Amongst my deepest wishes is that Spain had many moreleaders , such as Iker Casillas, Andrés Iniesta, Pau Gasol Rafa Nadal and Fernando Alonso who have made it to the top and have obtained international recognition thanks to their own effort, in every field of life such as music, literature, sports, science, business or finance. I have always tried to be a winner. I have never accepted a plan which was not based on the victory. That is why I understand and admire winners

PRINCIPLE #110: Digital Prosperity starts with this…

A WRITTEN GOAL…..

A goal which is not written is just a wish.

PRINCIPLE #111: Do the same as Bill Gates

Bill Gates did not watch TV Monday to Friday

PRINCIPLE #112: Be significantly successful

Success is when I add value to myself.
Significance is when I add value to Others.

PRINCIPLE #113: Feed your digital subconscious positively

You must keep your digital 2.0 subconcious mind fed AT ALL TIMES with positive thoughts so that their strong vibrations will ward off all negative and destructive thoughts from the outside 1.0 world.

PRINCIPLE #114: Teach Christianity to your Children using digital tools

We recommend you to use digital tools as parents to teach your children Christian values and pray that their faith will keep them while growing through the teenage years. Sometimes, even in Christmas families children vary from their faith But if the parents stay true to their own faith and continue to love and support their teens during their struggles, they often return to their roots and faith

PRINCIPLE #115: Learn to think before you feel

" The job of thinking is to clarify perception... In practice it is extremely difficult to think first and feel second. The overwhelming tendency is to feel first and then use thinking to back and support the feeling" Edward De Bono

PRINCIPLE #116: Use your digital mind as Mr/Ms. Success

Your digital mind is a "thought factory". It is a busy factory producing countless digital thoughts in one day. Production in your thought factory is under the charge of two digital folks, Mr(s) Success and Mr(s) Failure. Mr(s) Success is in charge of manufacturing digital positive thoughts. He specializes in producing reasons why you can, why you are qualified why you will. The only wise thing to do is to fire Mr(s) Failure. You do not need him/her digitally.

PRINCIPLE #117: Adopt the right digital attitude v others

It may suprise you to learn that in many of the cases in which you were treated discourteously digitally, where someone acts unreasonably towards you digitally, that you may have asked for that treatment. **You have to adopt the digital attitude you want others to express.**

PRINCIPLE #118: Picture your own digital creations

The power of picture works when you focus on what you want to create, not what you want to get rid of. Power Point itself as soon as you put the right words produces beautiful pictures which you can then save as JPEG

PRINCIPLE #119: Apply 3 basic steps daily

3 steps to self confidence

- Choose happiness as your number one goal
- Learn to trust yourself
- Use mental picturing to achieve your goals

PRINCIPLE #120: Be a person of values

Values are the beliefs that drive our behaviour

PRINCIPLE #121: Be a digital sprinter

We must learn to live our own lives as a series of digital sprints- fully engaging for periods of time, and then fully disengaging and seeking renewal before jumping back digitally into the fray to face whatever challenges confront us.

PRINCIPLE #122: Set a clear digital direction for your life

During the Industrial Age days. the average person´s life consisted of 20 years of having parents ask where he or she is going, 40 years of having a spouse ask the same question, and at the end, the mourners wondering the same. With the Digital Age you can overcome all obstacles easily as well as to accelerate the timings of your success.

PRINCIPLE #123: Digital Step by Digital Step

Goals are crucial but if you understand this: Digital Step by Digital Step. I cannot conceive any other way to achieve things. I have always set short-term goals rather than vague long-term goals. When I look back, I realise that each of those steps or partial successes took me to the next one.

PRINCIPLE #124:
Understanding your 4.0 leadership Internet capacity

Internet can be a control tool in the hands of the governments, but it can even be a more powerful tool in the hands of citizens committed to defend their democratic rights. If that all is true, what most people fail to see is that if a computer is used to generate wealth, you become a leader 4.0 in the IoT world. Just look at the number of leadership companies we have founded around the world.

PRINCIPLE #125: Talk to yourself repeatedly and loudly

Repetition : You need to repeatedly express your desires to your subconcious to your self-talk, until you achieve what you want.

PRINCIPLE #126: Turn 1.0 problems into digital 4.0 opportunities

Every obstacle is an opportunity.

PRINCIPLE #127: Start your millionaire DIGITAL QUEST

In the 10 years from 1991 to 2001, the number of US. Millionaire houselholds doubled from 3.6 Million to 7.2 Million. In the 10 years from 2006 to 2016 number doubled by creating another 10 million millionaires, for a total of more than 185 million millionaires!. By 2025 the number will be obviously much bigger.

PRINCIPLE #128: Being in digital business is a must

Remember that our digital business does not protect you from life, it just leaves you armed for it digitally.

PRINCIPLE #129: Fill your happiness digital bucket

Each of us has a digital bucket. It is constantly emptied or filled, depending on what others say or do to us. When our digital bucket is full, we feel great.

PRINCIPLE #130: Your digital enthusiasm is your IQ

Digital enthusiasm makes things 1100% per cent better. Interest, enthusiasm is the critical factor even in science ! With a positive, optimistic, and classy digital attitude a person with an IQ of 100 will earn more money, win more respect, and achieve more sucess than a negative, pesimistic, unco-operative individual with an IQ of 120

PRINCIPLE #131: Self-repeat a positive statement 20 times

Put a positive statement in writing and repeat it 21 times each go until it becomes permanent in your mind

PRINCIPLE #132: If you want true success, get out of the Corporate World

The Corporate world leaders are full of ego and do not how to lead. Working for them will never ever make you a leader. Leadership is not positionship.

PRINCIPLE #133: Act on your self-created emotions

Emotions do not just happen : you and only you create your own emotions and when this has occurred you have only one option left : you must act on them so that it when it comes to stronger emotions you are able to master them

.

PRINCIPLE #134: Don´t cheat yourself with nutrition

You are what you eat.

..

PRINCIPLE #135: Make every day a success

Where there is a will there is a way

PRINCIPLE #136: Managed solitude pays off

Successful digital leaders tap their super power through being alone, thus beating the Mr. I can´t-stand-be-alone who is unfortunately, ignorant of the digital superpower, lying unused just behind his forehead. Managed digital solitude pays off. Use it to release your creative power. Use it to find solutions to personal and business problems. So spend some time alone every day just for digital thinking. Use the thinking technique all great leaders use. Confer with yourself.

I

PRINCIPLE #137: Self-talk your self-program for digital success

After examining the philosophies, the theories and the practiced methods of influencing human behaviour, you will be delighted to learn the simplicity of one small fact: You become what you think most about: *your success or failure in anything, large or small, will depend on your programming –what you accept from others, and what you say when you talk to yourself.* It is no longer a success theory, it is a simple but powerful fact. Neither luck or desire has the slightest thing to do with it. It makes no difference whether we believe it or not. *The brain simply believes what you tell it most. And what you tell it about you, it will create. It has no choice. This guarantees your digital success.*

PRINCIPLE #138: Your children are the most important people

Treat the members of your family as the very important people they are, the most important in the world. Each morning go out into the digital world with the kind of attitude you would have if you were the most important person on earth thanks to them.

.

PRINCIPLE #139:Become a vitamin consumer

You might have become over-tired or be suffering from a simple kind of mild depresion that a simple course of vitamins could remedy. I used to weight 120 kg and have lost 40 over the years thank to proper vitamins

PRINCIPLE #140: Use your brain to eliminate nerves

The brain weighs 90% of the central nervous system. Therefore if you digitally educate it in leadership you will be ahead of 90% or more of the rest of the people.

PRINCIPLE #141: FOCUS, it is so simple

Follow

One

Course

Until

Successful

Negative digital answers tend to shut down and depress you. Positive digital answers tend to motivate you and give you confidence.

PRINCIPLE #142: Problems make you persistent

Understand there is no much difference between failure and success. Take time to write down your dream and the reason why you desire to fulfill it. Then write down all of the things that you would be willing to do digitally to make it happen. Try to think of everything that could possibly go wrong as you pursue it. **If you do that you will be mentally prepared for problems to come**. **And that will help you to be more persistent and be a worldwide winner digitally.**

PRINCIPLE # 143 Avoid ugly digital wording which affects your blood pressure

Certain digital words impact on your emotional intensity. If someone has lied to you and you used the words furious, livid or enraged, your physiology and your subsequent behaviour would be dramatically be altered. Your blood pressure would rise. Your face would turn beet red. You would feel tense all over. For example. complaints about the weather will not change the conditions. It simply makes no sense to get upset about things which have no control- and which have no significant impact in your life. The same applies to digital relationships. Leadership is all about people.

PRINCIPLE #144: Digital Winners are ex-losers

Digital Winners are just ex-losers who got mad. The battle belongs to the persistent. The victory will go to the one who does not quit ! Refuse to let friends or circumstances defeat you. You are finished when you are defeated...you are finished when you quit Confidence does not come out of nowhere. It is a result of something..hours and days and weeks and years of constant work and digital dedication. Act as if what you do makes a difference. It does .Enthusiasm is contagious. Start an epidemic. Prepare. The time to win your battle is before it starts. You are about to experience a turning point digitally. Stay in the game-it is too soon to quit.

PRINCIPLE #145: Water resolves many problems

Water absorbs negativity. This is another reason it is important to drink more water. To keep the energy flowing and to get the benefits of regular meditation, it is important to drink 8 to 10 glasses of water a day. If you are a bigger person, you will need more. To let go of anxiety I do this little process I ask myself what I am afraid of. Then I ask myself : Do I know for sure that those things will happen ? This frees me to see that when I am uncertain, I also have no certainty that anything bad will happen. Most anxiety is believing our fear (false evidence accepted as real) instead of remembering what we really do not know. By opening your mind to all possibilities, you can begin to tap into your inner guidance and to feel trust again.

PRINCIPLE #146: Your success is based on how you handle failure

The true measure of a man, it has been said, is not how he handles success. His real worth is determined by how he handles failure. Most of us have more experience with failure ; we learn from our mistakes, we dust ourselves off, and we get back into the fray. **But what happens when we have reached levels of achievement that allows us to do whatever we wish? Think about it and picture yourself succeeding digitally.**

PRINCIPLE #147: See yourself as leader

Most people think of leadership as a position and therefore they do not see themselves as leaders. It is the other way round, leadership is not a noun but a verb, it is action and moving. That is why digitalization creates leaders. Because they act and move daily in the digital arena.

PRINCIPLE #148: Digital Pep-talk

To be on top you´ve to feel you are on top. Give yourself a pep talk digitally and discover how much bigger and stronger your feel. Build a sell-yourself-to-yourself digital commercial. Remind yourself at every opportunity that you are a first-class digital person

.

PRINCIPLE #149: Give up the grudge poison

Give up the grudge in digital terms.
Grudges are **internal poisons** that harm the individual who holds them far more than they affect the actual object of the hatred. Every minute that you hang on to digital resentment is damaging you physically, mentally, emotionally and spiritually. In addition, when you dwell on anger and resentment, you « block » your mind´s creativity for digital ideas. Ideas flow best when you are calm and peaceful – not when you are consumed with hatred or revenge. **The bottom line is that your grudge is accomplishing nothing other than making you sick rather than digitally healthy.**

PRINCIPLE #150: You can and you will say you did it

Today I still listen to « We can » (PODEMOS) and Euro 2008 victory memmories come to my head. I wish the victory repeat and I wish it will be in South Africa. And I wish that after that World Cup another book can be written about the feat to tell that there, in South Africa, WE ALSO DID IT (PUDIMOS) « Iker Casillas, Spanish captain)

(from a Spanish writer whose words turned out to be true)

As a result Jorge Zuazola, already a founder of Spanish Leadership, went on to found American Leadership, German Leadership and European Leadership

www.ingramcontent.com/pod-product-compliance
Lightning Source LLC
Chambersburg PA
CBHW072247170526
45158CB00003BA/1026